SUNSHINE FOREVER

AN ANTHOLOGY OF POEMS

JAYASREE ASOK

ISBN 979-888530197-8

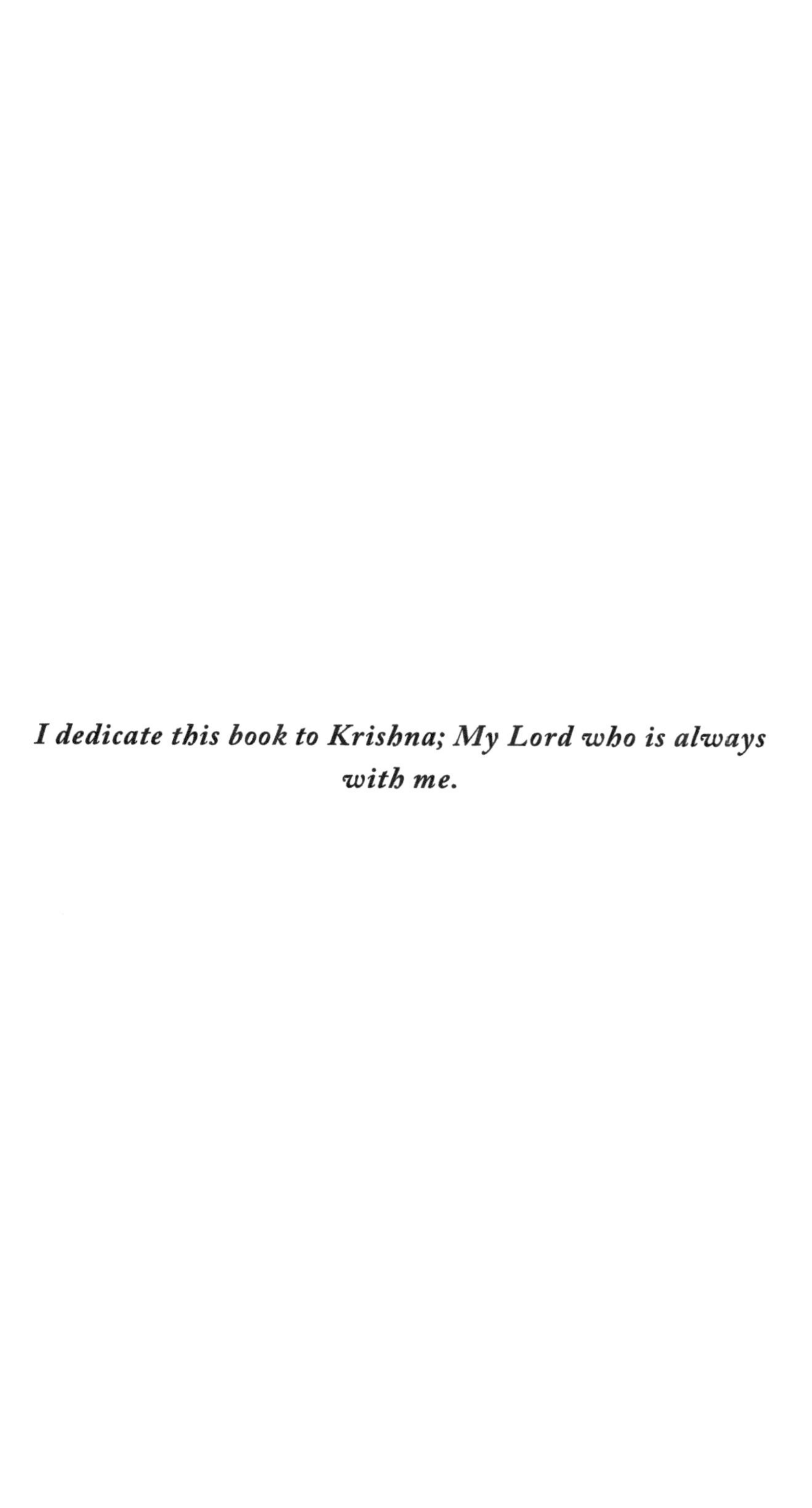

I dedicate this book to Krishna; My Lord who is always with me.

Contents

Foreword *ix*

Preface *xi*

Acknowledgements *xiii*

Prologue *xv*

1. Twilight 1
2. Krishna 2
3. Bud 3
4. Vadakkumnathan 4
5. Me 5
6. Memories 7
7. Sunshine Forever 8
8. Monsoon 9
9. Butterfly 10
10. Chasing The Rainbow 11
11. The Night Sky 12
12. The Cat In The Window 13
13. The Blue Planet 15
14. Forest 17
15. The Sound Of Music 18
16. Hope 19
17. The Earth Is Healing 20
18. Never Too Late 22
19. Little Gems 24
20. The Green Moth 26
21. Whispering Dreams 28
22. A Quilt Of Memories 29

Contents

23. Winter In Bahrain 30

24. Blessings 32

25. My Wish 33

26. The Frangipani Tree 34

27. Live And Let Live 35

28. The Party In The Forest 37

29. Cleansing The Mind 40

30. The Friendship Tree 42

31. Autumn 44

32. Of Insects, Birds And Animals 45

33. Night Over The Desert 47

34. The Falling Colours 48

35. From My Heart 50

36. The Walk 52

37. Words 53

38. Change The World 54

39. Frozen Dreams 55

40. Riding The Clouds 56

41. The Journey 57

42. Weep No More 59

43. The World Of Books 60

44. The Sound Of Silence 62

45. Feelings 63

46. A September Afternoon 64

47. Sunflowers In The Morning Sunshine 65

48. Flowers In The Rain 66

Contents

49. Eulogy For Ammini 67

50. Gratitude 69

51. The Sun, Sea And The Sky 70

Foreword

The proceeds from the sale of this book will be given to and shared equally between SOLACE, Thrissur, an organisation giving financial and emotional support to children with terminal illness (solaceglobal.org) and also to PAWS,(pawsthrissur.com) an organisation for the welfare of animals. These organisations are run by a dedicated and hardworking team of volunteers guided and led by Sheeba Ameer of SOLACE and Preethi Sreevalsan of PAWS.

Preface

I have always wanted to write, but found my niche only now, in my late fifties. My childhood and teens were spent reading and dreaming. The few poems that I wrote when I was a teenager, harbouring romantic dreams, never saw the light of the day. Being emotional and sensitive, even small things or incidents affect me. I am tuned to be aware of even the smallest things happening around me.

Writing these poems and making it into a book was a dream come true for me, something which happened only beacause of my Krishna's blessings.

I sincerely hope and pray that reading these poems will bring the same joy to you, that I felt while writing them.

Acknowledgements

To Asok, my soul mate, my better half. If not for you, my dream of writing would never have been realised. Thanks for encouraging me, for giving me the courage and confidence to share with others whatever I had jotted down in my note book. Thanks for being there for me always. A big thank you to my loving family and friends.

Love you all.

Prologue

'Turn your face to the Sun and the shadows fall behind you'

Old Maori proverb.

1. Twilight

Perched on the windowsill,
I watched the Sun setting
The shadows deepening
Twilight falling
The dusk painting the sky
in myriad hues.
There's a longing in me
A poignant desire
To hold on to the last of the Sun's rays.

2. Krishna

Krishna the Eternal one,
I bow before You
The ethereal music
from Your flute
floats across the mountains
The tinkling of the cowbells
echoes across the valley
And in the golden sunlight
I see you in all Your glory.
I am lost in Your
mesmerizing eyes
Your mischievous smile.
Krishna, what magic you weave!
All the paths I walk on
lead to You
All the thoughts I have
begin and end with You!
I follow You into eternity
I am lost in You
Lost in Your Aura.

3. Bud

In a shadowed green glade
In the middle of the forest
A tiny bud waits
To unfurl its velvety petals
To spread its fragrance
Its tiny face turned up to the blue skies
Waiting for the first kiss of the Sun's rays.

4. Vadakkumnathan

Walking barefoot along
the well trodden paths
Surrounded by the
dense foliage of the banyan trees
Immersed in the holy ambience
of this beautiful Temple
I am at peace with myself.
The dusk lit up with a
thousand oil lamps,
the air thick with the
fragrance of incense sticks
reverberating with the sound of drums
the temple bells and blowing conch
The flickering light of the oil lamps
light up the sanctum
I see the Lord,
the radiance that shines forth
And I bow my head before the Almighty.

5. Me

Who am I?
Am I
Just a speck
in the Universe?
I soar high
above the clouds
I dive deep into the seas
Trying to find myself
searching and seeking.
Is it me
flying on the
gossamer wings
of the butterfly?
Is it me
mirrored on the
petals of the flower
drenched in the morning dew?
Is it me
flying on the
wings of the wind
that blows past the mountains?
Is it me,
riding the waves that
break on sandy shores.

Is it me
floating on the clouds
in the blue blue sky....
I try to find myself
searching and seeking
I try to find the real me
To be one with nature
To be eternally free!

6. Memories

Memories like clouds floating along
in the sky of my mind
Sometimes bright and beautiful
like a sunny day
filling me up with happiness
lighting me up from within.
At times clouding them dark
like purple rain clouds ready to burst
and spill out as tears from my eyes.

7. Sunshine forever

Sunlight falls
like a bouquet of flowers
turning the dust motes
into spun gold.
The golden dust
floating down,
spills onto the trees and flowers
onto the grass
bathing everything
in its golden glow.
I hold a drop of the
golden Sun in my palms
shining forever.

8. Monsoon

They come without fail, year after year.
The cool breeze a prelude to the rain...
The dark purple clouds
filled with raindrops
ready to fill the earth with hope;
hope of escaping the summer
the ever pervasive heat;
the humid blanket that smothers,
bringing relief to the parched earth
hope of new life sprouting.
The monsoon is here!
Waking up in the morning
to the music of the rains
to the smell of freshly washed earth.
Afternoons heavy with rain filled clouds,
the dark evenings filled with rain;
the nights alive with the sound of cicadas
and the whisper of the rain fly's wings
as they rise up from the damp earth.
The monsoon is here, bringing with it
the music of the rains.

9. Butterfly

With wings translucent and bright
It flutters from flower to flower
soaking up the warm sunshine
gliding on the rising wind.....
A tiny butterfly
shining like a jewel
forever beautiful!

10. Chasing The Rainbow

Futile the efforts
chasing the rainbow
always eluding,
always outside your grasp;
the colours that be fading away
never to be touched
the pot of gold still elusive...
Then, as you flounder
disappointment clouding over
you realize you are the rainbow
shining with all the vibrant colours
the elusive pot of gold is within you
not yet unearthed
The colours that be
fill your soul to make you whole.

11. The Night Sky

A full moon hangs low
like a lantern
lighting up the night sky.
The haunting music
of night birds
wafts across the still air.
A soft wind kisses
the tops of the trees
and the fragrance of
night blooming jasmine
fills the moonlit night.
A million stars
sparkling like diamonds
adorn the sky.
And I stand
lost in the wonder
of the silver-soaked night..
The moonlight
shimmering and glittering
all around me.

12. The Cat In The Window

She sits on the window ledge
watching the world.
I wonder what's on her mind.
Is she looking
at the woods beyond
at what dangers lurk there
Is she worrying about
how to survive in this world
Is she sad, thinking
about her lost kittens
worrying about her
one surviving baby
or is she having some 'me' time
away from all her problems
watching the
bees and the butterflies,
wondering what's beyond
the blue blue sky.
Or, is she thinking
of what mischief
she can get away with.
She sits there
on the window ledge
warming herself

in the sunlight
still ... not moving
She sits on the window ledge
watching the world.

13. The Blue Planet

Somewhere along the way
compassion is lost
Humanity, empathy
buried deep down
never to surface.
Wars raging on
People killing people
Earth, our beautiful planet
pillaged and plundered
Our home
filled with everything dear
slowly deteriorating
Waste mountains springing up
dwarfing even the mightiest
Seas choking with debris
The world slowly changing
Green valleys giving way
to rocky slopes
Forests slowly disappearing;
mutilated and benumbed
the animals, homeless
dying one by one
The sea crying silently
Its creatures choking and dying

The Earth is changing
What we had is no more
Wake up! before it's too late
care for our world
Our beautiful blue planet.

14. Forest

The dark green forest
beckons me!
Sunlight falling through
the dense branches
drawing patterns
on the forest floor;
on the fallen leaves...
I walk along the
leaf strewn paths,
the dew soaked leaves
wet under my bare feet.
The music of the chirping birds
and cicadas serenading me...
I touch the wild flowers
I touch the touch me nots
I see them curling up like babies
And my heart sings!
This is bliss, to be alive
in such a beautiful world.

15. The Sound Of Music

The distant sound of music
floats in from afar..
It touches a chord in my heart
The notes play on the
strings of my heart
The melodies soothe me
The nostalgic memories
crowd in
washing up like waves
on the shores of my mind
evoking feelings deeply buried,
taking me to another world.
And I escape into the music
until there's just me
and my music
and my memories.

16. Hope

The tear drops I shed
fall like pearls
in my mind
and washes away
the sadness within.
A ray of hope
shining golden,
lights up my soul
and I weave an
intricate tapestry
of hope and happiness
adorned with
golden thread and pearls
to be hung forever in my mind.

17. The Earth Is Healing

People confined
Never stepping out
Distancing themselves
confused and scared;
Panic in their eyes
like trapped animals
in cages.
The price we pay
for our atrocities
for our wrongdoings!
And amidst
the chaos and confusion
nature starts healing.
The earth starts
breathing again;
fresh air
flowing through mountains,
polluted rivers and oceans.
Burnt forests
sprouting new leaves!
The earth is healing,
slowly and silently.
Is the pandemic
which wrought

havoc everywhere
nature's way of reclaiming
what it has lost?
New life, New hopes!

18. Never Too Late

As the years pass by
I realise what I lost
and what I gained.
So many things
left undone,
opportunities lost...
The silence in between,
words unspoken,
sentences not written,
the pauses in between
too long!
And in the fine line
between night and morning
I wake up and realise
what I was,
was never enough
what I was,
was not whole.
Time flies,
never comes back.
I am encased in a bubble
Regrets
clouding my thoughts!
Then one fine day

the bubble burst,
the regrets fled
and I realised that
life is a blessing.... God's gift!
It's never too late for anything
never too late to bloom!

19. Little Gems

Each time I step into my class
the wonder never ceases
the wonder of being able
to mould and teach the little ones
Buds waiting to bloom and blossom!
Each year when I meet them
the girls and boys with their
well scrubbed clean faces
and combed hair
their innocent faces
looking up at me with love
looking up at me expectantly
waiting for me to love them
encourage them
their heart full of love
innocence pooled in their eyes
I feel the wonder of God.
Each one different
some artistic
some studious, some naughty
some shy, each child unique!
I treasure each moment;
the flowers I got;
the small trinkets

made with their little hands
just for me;
little notes of love
pressed into my hand
shyly and silently;
the way the scared ones
put their soft little hands
into mine
looking for reassurance,
their wide eyed wonder
at everything they see and hear
their look of joy
when I open a story book
to take them into another world.
They are precious gems
to be cut and polished,
to shine forever!
Bringing happiness
to them and to others.
All they need is Tender Loving Care

20. The Green Moth

The moth
delicate and beautiful
sits on the kitchen floor
Her fragile filigree wings
fluttering, trying hard to fly
to escape
looking for a safe place
to lay the eggs she's carrying.
Must have come in
during the night
seeking warmth and light.
I hold her in my palm
coaxing her to fly...
She flutters her pale green wings
not flying
just a soft flutter
and then
as I take her and put her
amongst the plants and trees
in her natural surroundings,
like a miracle on wings
with a soft whisper
of her wings
she flies from tree to tree

plant to plant
seeking a safe home
for her babies.
Even a small being as a moth
has her survival instincts!
Set them free
all of nature's creatures...
to live freely
to let the cycle of life continue
That's the rule of nature!

21. Whispering Dreams

Dreams embellished with magic
falling like stars all around me
dreams whispering
filling my whole being
lending me wings to fly
taking me to places not seen
I dream on and on
with eyes open
eyes closed...
I cross deep forests
dark and mysterious...
I walk through valleys
filled with sun kissed flowers,
climb mist covered mountains,
glide through puffy white clouds,
climb rainbows....
I cross seas and oceans
wade through streams
following my dreams
I dream on and on
my mind wistful...
Dreams...
giving me hope to go on!

22. A Quilt Of Memories

I stitch memories
with the thread of time
Some happy
Some sad
Some nostalgic.
Memories that
blanket my life
in a colourful quilt!

23. Winter In Bahrain

The subtle changes;
A chill in the air
dusk approaching early
days shorter, nights longer
and winter, on it's way.
A while back
seeing the woollens in the mall
I wondered
at the winter clothes
here in Bahrain, in the Gulf
where there's only scorching summers!
Silly me; me who knows
only the summer heat and the
monsoon rains of the tropics
the winter is unknown;
A novel experience!
Then come November
as the temperature dropped
there's a glow in my heart
warming me up...
The excitement of a season
not yet experienced.
The winter with its
cold chilly mornings and nights,

freezing winds;
And the mist creeping in
from the Arabian sea is here...
And I
wrapped up in my winter wear
a softly humming heater
and a mug of hot chocolate
warming me up,
snuggled cozily by the window,
reveled in the happiness
winter evoked in me...
As everything unique
in this beautiful tiny Island
Even in winter the sun shone down
golden and bright every day
and the stars twinkled
in a clear night sky.
The sky, blue and cloudless,
the light so intense, that
the first winter in Bahrain was the best.

24. Blessings

I am blessed and am thankful.
But why then
is my heart filled with longing;
Why is my mind restless
seeking and searching
for something
like a weary traveller
seeking an oasis
in the endless desert of life...
Why don't I realise that
life is a mirage ...
Why am I lost
in the musings
of a wandering soul
restless, my heart fluttering
like a bird in a cage...
I know not.
I just know that I should do my best.
For I am blessed
and I thank the lord for all the blessings.

25. My Wish

Imagination running wild
the heights, the places
it takes me to
guides me to
find a niche for myself
a space for me
to escape to.
I wish
it never ends
the magic that words weave.
I wish
the wells of ink
never dries up
I wish
my pen,
my magic wand
sprinkles the magic dust
on my poems.
I wish
I could keep on writing.....

26. The Frangipani Tree

On a small hill
silhouetted against
the night sky
stands a lone frangipani tree.
Its branches weighed down
with buds,
ready to bloom!
As the crescent moon rises
in the horizon
and the silver moonlight
touches the waiting buds,
they unfurl their
yellow-white petals softly,
spreading intoxicating fragrance
all around the still night air
as they bloom and blossom....
The flowers fully bloomed
luminescent and exotic,
glow like lit lamps
on the lone tree
silhouetted against
the night sky!

27. Live And Let Live

Ensconced in a cocoon
watching the world go by
a world changing
for the better...
The bruises
slowly healing
a time to reflect,
think and act.
A lesson learnt
to restrain ourselves;
Spaces marked
never to be crossed over;
A lesson learnt
to realise our mistakes
to share the world selflessly
with all the other creatures.
To live in harmony
To live and let live
The losses, the trials
making us stronger!
Walking over
new pathways
footsteps never faltering
embracing the changes....

Seeds of hope and kindness
sprouting in the
mind's garden;
Ready to emerge from the cocoon
like a beautiful butterfly...
To live and let live!

28. The Party In The Forest

Last night
there was a party in the forest
A midnight party!
Only the bugs and insects
and no one else ...
They worked hard
for it was a grand party
Each one doing their best...
The twinkling lights
set up by the fireflies
shining all through
the dark night...
The décor and colour
by the butterflies and dragonflies
all with their
vibrant wings fluttering!
The music?
Of course the music band
was all ready to rock!
The grasshoppers
in their green dress on the violin;
The cicadas and crickets
all dressed in brown
on the drums;

The centipedes and the millipedes
playing soft notes
on the piano;
The praying mantis with a guitar
strung across his shoulder
strumming softly
was all set to sing
at the top of his voice!
And the food ? OH Yes, the food;
The bees
in their black and yellow striped dress
brought the honey,
The marching ants
dressed all in red
brought the bread crumbs...
It was yummy, delicious!
The lady bugs
in their
red and black polka dotted dress
danced the night away!
And the wasps
with their stings ready,
stood guard so,
no one gatecrashed!!!
For the party was
just for the bugs and the insects...
So, how do I know
it was a great party..
because I was that little butterfly

fluttering in the blue and gold dress
dancing the night away
at the party in the forest,
my wings reflecting
the twinkling lights of the fireflies...

29. Cleansing The Mind

Mind bogged down
with emotional baggage
Seeped in the aftermath
of disquieting thoughts;
thoughts which glow like embers...
Despair clouding the mind;
A mind restless
searching for a safe haven...
A mind drowned
in a sea of emotions
trying to anchor itself!
A mind sad and lost!
And when everything seems
gloomy and dark...
Close your eyes,
meditate
And fill it with all things
beautiful in this world!
Plough the mind
ridding it of all things bad.
Pluck out the weeds of
discontent and hatred;
Plant the seeds of
good and happy thoughts,

Nurture it and watch
the miracle garden
of happy thoughts bloom
filling you with happiness ...

30. The Friendship Tree

Lush and green
proud and tall
stands the friendship tree;
Its wide branches
giving shade lovingly...
Its roots deep in the soil!
Time goes by
and the winds of change blows,
Old leaves fall
but never lost,
always there,
feeding the tree
making it stronger,
branches spread wider....
The new leaves sprout,
tender and green
filling the tree again and again..
And it goes on and on
The cycle continues,
the friendship tree
ever growing...
Old friends never leaving,
making you stronger
always with you.

Happiness, sorrow,
aspirations, fear
everything shared!
New friendships giving you
new hopes to go on,
making you feel young and vibrant!
Family, Friends!!
What would life be without them!

31. Autumn

With the changing colours of the season
in the palette of my mind
I mix the reds, yellows, browns and gold
mixing and spreading...
A stroke here, a swish there
And I paint the world inside me
with a million beautiful colours...

32. Of Insects, Birds And Animals

Born into this beautiful world
the innocent creatures that
live alongside us.
Each one beautiful and special
touched and blessed
by God's hands!
Born with a purpose
fulfilling their duties selflessly
these creatures
who cannot talk...
They are special!
Balancing our world,
giving selfless love!
The birds, the animals,
the insects;
the world lost without them...
Do the bees know,
without them
we are a lost race?
Do the butterflies realise
how pretty they are;
the happiness they spread?

Do the birds know the joy
they bring with
their sweet songs;
their beautiful plumage shining
in the early morning sunlight.
Do the animals realise
the part they play in our life;
some protecting
some bringing happiness,
loving us selflessly
maintaining the
balance of nature
going about their life
not harming anyone
except for their survival.
Do we,
the ignorant humans
know the part played
by these insects, birds and animals
in our survival?
We are nothing without them!
So love them, protect them,
they are precious...

33. Night Over The Desert

The desert shimmers silver
in the starlit night..
The night sky
like a crystal blanket
with the twinkling stars
sewn on it!
The silence of the night
broken by the whisper
of the blooming desert flowers,
the fluttering
of the night birds' wings,
and the sound of the
shifting sand dunes
in the wind.
The desert, a sea of sand
stretches endlessly
to the horizon
where the stars rain down
on the wild flowers
draping them in silver!

34. The Falling Colours

The rain fell in
great big drops
pitter-patter, pitter-patter
for days on end,
no respite
the days dark and gloomy
wet and grey...
A yearning
for the golden sun
warm, yellow and glowing....
A yearning
for the colours that
adorn nature
in all its splendour....
A wish to
fill the world with colour;
A wish heard... for, the sun
peeped through
the dark clouds
through the soft rain
and a rainbow was born!!
It touched
the drooping flowers
the huddling birds

the dragonflies and butterflies;
The falling colours
swirling and blending
filling everything
in its path...
And the world shone
colourful, bright and sparkling
in the soft sunlight,
in the falling rain.

35. From My Heart

A thousand thoughts,
yearnings,
milling around...
Thoughts that
churn in my mind.
Yearnings
an ache in my mind
Memories that
pave paths
to walk
on and on and on;
Memories that
refuse to let go
clinging to the walls
of my mind
nurtured by the tears
I shed.
Memories that
changed me forever!
I long for the old me,
for who I was...
I yearn to escape
from those sad memories
To remember

only the good ones
to be free and happy....
Mind tranquil
as a still pond.

36. The Walk

Walking through the meadows
where purple and yellow flowers bloom...
Walking through the valleys
where the soft breeze whisper and caress...
Walking on the sun dappled paths
carpeted with wild flowers...
Walking in the rain
the cool rain drops washing away the despair...
A walk to heal, to rejuvenate, to make everything all right!

37. Words

Words dancing around, filling my mind;
Words metamorphosing into butterflies
colourful and fluttering
their wings spread wide
ready to take flight,
to land on the blank pages of my book.
But hesitant and timid they hover
never settling, never still
and they fly away from my mind!
The pages not filled... A fleeting thought,
a word, a line, not captured
and pinned onto the blank pages...
Words liberated, fly away
free as the wind, free as the butterflies
never captured and pinned.

38. Change The World

I wish I had the power
to change the world;
To erase the grief
poverty, suffering, sickness...
To bring happiness
to everyone...
The power to spread
kindness and empathy.
I wish
I was a ray of sunlight,
a ray of hope
shining gold and pure
showing the right path...
A sliver of moonlight
lighting
up the dark path...
A crystal star shining
like a beacon of hope...

39. Frozen Dreams

My dreams twinkle like stars
in the sky of my mind,
longing for the daylight,
to be fulfilled...
Alas! they disappear
in the morning light
and the dreams inside me
remain locked...
Frozen and timeless.

40. Riding The Clouds

Riding the clouds
into the pink and orange sunset;
The last of the sun's rays
kissing my eyelids;
the gathering dusk
all around me...
The twilight hour resonating
with a stillness, the stillness
of the approaching night...
A lone star twinkling
in the evening sky,
showing me the way to heaven!
The night sky slowly dropping
a curtain of sparkling silver stars!
Riding the clouds into the silver starlit night.....

41. The Journey

A tiny drop of water
nestling in the raincloud,
waiting to fall
with the music of the rains.
Sometimes cradled
on a green leaf;
Sometimes
on a blooming flower,
before falling
onto the bosom
of the waiting earth...
Joining other raindrops,
forming rivulets...
Streams gushing and tinkling,
streams that flow
through rocky terrains,
beautiful valleys and deep forests
smoothening the pebbles.
The gurgling sound,
music in the silent forest...
The tiny rain drop
journeys on and on...
The stream becomes a river,
calm and serene, flowing silently

to reach it's goal, to be one
with the sea,
to kiss the grains of sand
on a golden beach
to wash up as waves on earth's bosom.

42. Weep No More

Why do you weep girl..
Why did they clip your wings
imprison your spirit...
Why do you weep woman..
Why did they torture you
Tear your tender body apart
like petals from a flower...
Is being born a girl
the only sin you committed?
Weep no more my child;
Weep no more woman;
for no fault of yours!
Raise your voice
and from your
bruised and tattered mind
shout out loud for all to hear!
Emboldened and empowered
rise up like a phoenix bird
from the ashes of suppression.

43. The World Of Books

The world of books!
Each new book opened
Each new page turned
opening up
a new path to walk on
a new world to explore.
Fying off on a magic carpet
to faraway places...
Sleeping in tree houses;
walking through
enchanted forests
where the magic fairies fly
with their sparkling wings!
Where elves help you
find your way...
Where talking animals
frolic and play!
Meeting epic heroes!
Brave warriors!
Solving mysteries, finding treasures...
A world enchanting, magical,
romantic and thrilling...
Each new day that dawns
filled with an adventure

Something to look forward to...
Years pass by
and the world changes
But books, still the same
as captivating as ever!
The intoxicating smell
of a new book
as nostalgic as ever!
The journey through
the world of books
goes on and on
Never tiring... Cherished
Held close to my soul...

44. The Sound Of Silence

The sound of silence,
the most melodious sound ever!
The sound of new life sprouting,
the tender shoot of a plant
shyly poking its head
into a new world.
A bud slowly opening its petals
A mushroom opening its umbrella
The sun rising and setting
The clouds sailing by
The rainbow smiling
The moonlight falling on the trees
The stars twinkling
The sound of the good earth
rejoicing life...
Make time to listen to the sound of silence.

45. Feelings

All that you feel and sense
All that you see and do
Colours your world...
The colours burst inside
filling the blank canvas of your mind
to evolve as a beautiful painting
that reflects you...

46. A September Afternoon

The golden rays
of the afternoon sun
fall through the
sun dappled trees.
The dragonflies glide
soaking up the sunlight,
their transparent wings
coloured golden,
enjoying their
tiny moment of happiness...
The air heavy
with the fragrance
of jasmine flowers,
drowsy with the
buzzing of the bees.
The earth still,
somnolent under
the afternoon sun...
And even in the stillness
there is life.

47. Sunflowers In The Morning Sunshine

Faces turned up adoringly
to the rising sun
soaking up the sun's rays
tinging their petals yellow
stands the sunflowers
row upon row, like
undulating waves of
yellow and green...
Golden sun drops fallen
from the sky,
they shimmer in the breeze.
Tall and beautiful, they stand,
the sunflowers
framed against an azure blue sky
like a beautiful painting...

48. Flowers In The Rain

Sleeping petals
woken up
by the gently falling rain...
Glistening raindrops
falling off
the unfurling petals...
Rain-soaked and dewy
the flower smiles
welcoming the rain
that fills her up!

49. Eulogy For Ammini

Old, sick, hungry and scared,
crying and whining
for her loved ones
she lay for days soaking wet,
in the relentless rain.
No one to care, no food, no water
abandoned; she waited....
Old and blind, her only fault...
A gentle, loving and docile creature.
How can people be
so cruel; so heartless
betraying the trust
of these mute beings...
Her only fault
she can't talk, but her heart
full of love, unselfish and whole...
Her faith in us constant
never doubting, that
she will be cared for!
Poor soul, her faith misplaced
for, she was abandoned...
Cruel and heartless
her owner left her
to fend for herself!

Thirsty and hungry
she whined and cried...
But, not all of God's children
are heartless and cruel
for she was found, fed,
cared and loved for...
She left this world yesterday
for God's abode
But before she left she got love at its best,
care and shelter, safety and warmth.
Ammini, the gentle loving soul
one among many who suffers like this!
But for people who care about them..
Our mute friends and all creatures
wonderful in this world.
But for them she would have died
hungry and scared
and all alone in the falling rain...
I have not met you Ammini
but I feel for you, my heart is heavy!
I pray you are happy, loved and safe
wherever you are!

50. Gratitude

Thought-waves come crashing
on to the rocky shores
of the mind
like endless waves
churning in the sea...
One after the other
they come, endless....
Breaking into a thousand shards
Seeping into everything...
Thought strands weaving a cobweb
from the past to the present.
Mind floundering
in the crashing waves,
trapped and tangled in the cobwebs,
trying to escape...
Still the mind... still the waves...
Dust the cobwebs...
Live in the present
the now, for it's a gift!
Gratitude filling the mind
for the beautiful memories that live inside...
And for the beautiful memories yet to come!

51. The Sun, Sea and the Sky

The sea dressed up in
myriad hues of blue,
the colours blending
and overlapping...
Calm and serene,
she hides a
teeming world
of coral reefs and fish
in her womb,
her gentle waves
rolling onto the
pristine white beaches,
bleached white
by the coral...
Adorned with fluffy clouds
tinted golden and pink
the sky,
holds onto the sea's hands,
never letting go..
With a beaming sun
looking on!
Sometimes bright
sometimes overcast
sometimes blue

and at times grey!
The sky changes;
the changing moods
flowing onto the sea.
Calm or turbulent
sunny or rainy
they are one...
merging on the horizon
forever and ever!

And so it ends, hoping and praying it's a start to many more happy endings yet to come!

Many thanks to you, dear reader!

9 798885 301978

Printed by Libri Plureos GmbH in Hamburg, Germany